INSIDE SPECIAL FORCES ™

SPECIAL OPS: SNIPERS

Mary-Lane Kamberg

rosen publishing's
rosen
central
New York

For Herbert R. Carter, LTC, USA, Ret.
Thank you for your service.

Published in 2015 by The Rosen Publishing Group, Inc.
29 East 21st Street, New York, NY 10010

First Edition

Library of Congress Cataloging-in-Publication Data

Kamberg, Mary-Lane, 1948–
Special ops: snipers/Mary-Lane Kamberg.
    pages cm.—(Inside Special Forces)
Includes bibliographical references and index.
ISBN 978-1-4777-7989-7 (library bound)—ISBN 978-1-4777-7990-3
(pbk.)—ISBN 978-1-4777-7991-0 (6-pack)
1. Sniping (Military science—United States—Juvenile literature. 2. Snipers—
United States—Juvenile literature. I. Title. II. Title: Snipers.
UD333.K36 2014
356'.162—dc23
                                                                2014023129

Manufactured in Malaysia

CONTENTS

INTRODUCTION

In 2006 a four-man U.S. sniper team set out on an information-gathering mission in Afghanistan. They were to watch a farmhouse the enemy was known to use as a meeting place. As always, the sniper team carried photos of wanted enemy leaders. If the team happened to see one of them, the snipers were authorized to take him out.

The carefully planned mission included several escape routes. An American infantry quick-response group would hide in the targeted area. So would another group whose job it was to help the snipers return to base at the end of the mission.

Just after dark, the four-man team left their home base on foot. They wore heavy ghillie suits that felt like leather jackets. (A ghillie suit is a disguise that helps snipers blend in with the area. It is covered with netting and plant fibers or vegetation.) The suits made the men sweat in the 95°F (35°C) air temperature. The suits also made the men itch. What's more, the suits often caught on branches and bushes. But they served the all-important purpose of keeping the team hidden.

Each man carried forty pounds (eighteen kilograms) of personal gear and a sixty-pound (twenty-seven-kilogram) equipment bag. One man had an M24 rifle with a 10-power scope. Another had a 40-power spotting scope that looked like a mini-telescope. He and the other two men also carried M14 rifles.

The team crossed the river over a log bridge. Because the roads were high enough that the soldiers would be silhouetted against the horizon, the team crouched along the lower edge of the road until they reached the cover provided by a group of date palms.

They walked all night, creeping over more than six miles (ten kilometers) of farmland. Still in darkness, they reached the small house. The sniper team members were tired and hungry, but they couldn't stop to rest or eat. They set up a hide, a firing position, hidden among a patch of ten-foot-high (three-meter-high) reeds on the side of a ditch about the length of four football fields from the house.

The soldier with the M24 aimed at the house while the one with the scope helped him observe the scene. Another used a radio to stay in touch with the team's commander. The fourth covered the rear of the position

Snipers often camouflage themselves by wearing ghillie suits, disguises made from vegetation from the area of operation. These specially crafted suits make the soldiers blend in with their environment.

for added security. They watched the house for about an hour as dawn broke. Finally, a man came out of the house and walked over to his neighbor's home. The man looked like one of the targeted enemy leaders. However, all the team had was a grainy computer printout of his picture. The team couldn't identify him for sure, and so, held back.

The radioman contacted their commander, and the team watched and waited among the reeds for another three hours. The team observed the suspect assembling an improvised explosive device (IED), a homemade bomb that could be left on the side of a road to kill unsuspecting travelers, in this case, American soldiers. Soon a pickup truck pulled into the yard, and the suspect climbed in. Fearing he would get away, one of the snipers fired at the truck.

Because the sniper team was well hidden, the men in the truck had no idea where the shot had come from. They scrambled out of the truck, hands up. The quick-reaction force, which had been waiting on the sidelines, sped onto the scene and captured the man.

The sniper team followed the drainage ditch to the road, entered the infantrymen's tracked M113 armored personnel carrier, and returned to base. The mission, which was typical of a sniper team's job, had been long, hot, and tiring. It was also successful. The prisoner did turn out to be the suspected enemy leader. However, the sniper team members were glad that they waited for positive identification and hadn't killed the wrong man.

CHAPTER 1

WHAT SNIPERS DO

They crouch on rooftops in cities and settle into vegetation in the countryside. Hidden from view, they lie in wait. They watch everything. Ordinary people going about their day. Enemy movement. Stockpiles of weapons and supplies. The goal is "to see without being seen" and "kill without being killed."

They are snipers.

Military snipers are expert shooters who use long-range weapons from a hidden position. They have extra training in disguise, observation, and movement. Although they sometimes must kill enemy soldiers, they do so to protect their fellow soldiers in combat situations.

Snipers work in such areas as jungles, forests, and cities. They work alone or in teams of two or more to observe the enemy or to fire on selected human or material targets. They hope to hit the target with one shot and escape without being exposed.

The term *sniper* was first used by British soldiers in India in the 1770s. It described a hunter who could bag a wading game bird called a snipe. The snipe is known for being hard to hunt. Its natural coloring makes it hard to see in a marsh. And the unpredictable way it flies makes it hard to hit in the air. A man who could hit a snipe was a fine shooter, indeed. About fifty years later, *sniper* was first used in the military sense to describe a highly accurate shooter who fires from a hidden place.

OBSERVATION AND COVER

Today, every branch of the U.S. military uses snipers. Their primary mission is to support combat operations. They fire precise, long-range shots on selected enemies or targeted objects.

The word sniper *originally referred to an expert hunter who could kill a snipe, a well-camouflaged wading bird with a long, slender bill and an unpredictable flight pattern.*

Snipers create enemy casualties, slow enemy movement, frighten and confuse enemy soldiers, and lower their morale. Snipers are considered high-precision weapons—valuable assets in combat.

The sniper's secondary job is to collect and report battlefield information. The team observes and reports on the strength, equipment, and location of enemy forces. Team members use all five senses but mostly rely on sight and sound. They first do a hasty visual search of an area. They use binoculars to glance at places the enemy could hide. They start closest to their firing position and move their vision farther away in quick looks. A detailed search follows with closer observation of the area. A hasty search followed by a detailed search is repeated three or four times to give the sniper a good idea of what the area contains.

At times, a sniper team simply observes an area and reports back to its unit. At other times, the team provides over-watch, a type of support that includes observing the battlefield and providing covering fire for friendly units.

Despite the high-tech nature of modern warfare, snipers remain important on the battlefield. They can take out targets without collateral damage, unnecessary damage to civilians. This ability is especially needed on peacekeeping missions.

WORKING AS A TEAM

Snipers may work alone, but they usually train and work in pairs. One sniper is the team leader; the other is the observer, or spotter. Some teams include such additional members as communications personnel and extra security.

The spotter selects a target and helps the shooter estimate the distance to it. The spotter also figures out the effects of existing weather conditions and gives the lead sniper the information. The lead sniper builds or chooses the firing position and identifies the target. He adjusts his aim for wind, elevation, and other effects. Before firing a shot, he tells the spotter he's ready.

Snipers usually work in teams comprised of a spotter and a shooter, such as these U.S. Marines during the war in Vietnam.

KEY SNIPER TARGETS

Choosing a target is an important part of the spotter's job. He may identify personnel, weapon systems, or other equipment. Some key enemy targets include:

- Snipers

- Dog-tracking teams

- Scouts

- Officers and noncommissioned officers

- Vehicle drivers

- Communications personnel

- Weapon crews

- Optical equipment on closed vehicles

- Communication and radar equipment

- High-tech and computer-guided weapon systems

The spotter observes the shot. He looks for swirl, the bullet's vapor trail. He also looks for splash, dirt, or other material kicked up by a bullet that hits the ground. After the first shot, the lead sniper prepares to fire another one if needed. If the shot missed, the observer tells the shooter how to adjust his aim.

A sniper's combat role differs from that of foot soldiers, who also participate in gunfights with enemy military units. For one thing, the sniper seldom fires more than two shots from the same position. More than that makes it too easy for the enemy to see the sniper and to shoot back. For another, unlike soldiers in a firefight who aim at any available target, the sniper usually zeroes in on a specific one.

Snipers evaluate potential targets in terms of their threat to the sniper team the chances of hitting the target with one shot how certain the sniper is of the target's identity and the effect on the

A scout sniper observation telescope, such as the one used in this U.S. Marine training mission, gives spotters a close-up view of a target that may be a mile or more away.

enemy, as well as what the enemy will likely do after the shot is taken. Probably most important is the effect that taking a shot will have on the sniper's overall mission.

HIDE AND SEEK

Snipers need more than accurate marksmanship. They must be masters of fieldcraft, namely, being able to work undetected even when they are in open country. Snipers must also know how to stalk quietly and effectively. On the battlefield, stalking means sneaking up on an enemy or getting in position to observe, and if necessary, fire. Snipers must use patience and move slowly with purpose. They must select each new position in terms of how they will get there and whether they will have enough cover when they do.

Sometimes snipers lie in the same position for hours or days to wait for a target or to observe enemy activities. During that time, they must disguise themselves. They use several types of camouflage, alone or in combination. They hide behind an object or settle into thick vegetation. They try to blend in with the area by concealing their body by wearing clothing with coloring that matches the surroundings.

Snipers may use natural materials that are native to the area or such artificial materials as camouflage sticks or face paint to cover exposed skin. They often wear ghillie suits, specialized clothing originally created for deer hunting in

TARGET INDICATORS

Snipers must avoid becoming targets themselves. To do that, they must know and avoid target indicators that can give away their location. A target indicator is anything that could result in detection. Snipers must take great care not to do anything that reveals their position and makes them an enemy target.

Target indicators include:

- Sounds, be they from movement, talking, or the rattle of equipment

- The sight of quick or jerking motion—slow movement is harder to see

Scotland's highlands. Gamekeepers used them as portable hunting blinds to keep such game as deer and ducks from detecting the hunter.

Military snipers wear the suits so they can both move about free of detection and hide in a firing position. The human form is the most easily recognized shape on the planet. Ghillie suits create a three-dimensional pattern to disguise the human outline.

- Such improper camouflage as reflection, contrast with the area, and skylining (the outline of the person seen above the horizon)

- Smells, such as from soap, lotion, or insect repellent

- Such wildlife activities as birds suddenly taking flight or the sudden silence of animal sounds

- Overhead movement of trees, bushes, or tall grasses caused by rubbing against them

A U.S. Marine sniper team sets up a rooftop firing position during Operation Iraqi Freedom. The spotter's clothing contrasts with the background, making him a too-easy enemy target.

15

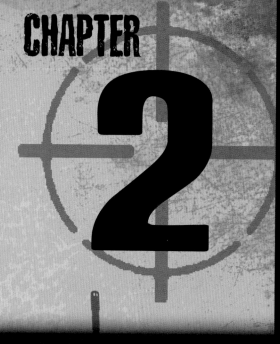

CHAPTER 2

A STORIED PAST

O ne of the earliest-known American sniper actions occurred in 1777 in the Battle of Bemis Heights during the Revolutionary War. British forces from Canada were trying to defeat American troops in upstate New York. British general Simon Fraser led an advance unit into the area.

On the American side, General Daniel Morgan led a team of riflemen known as Morgan's Sharpshooters, including Timothy Murphy, an American frontiersman known for his shooting accuracy. The general wanted to upset the enemy's leadership and leave the rest of the enemy soldiers afraid and confused. He ordered Murphy to take out the British general.

Hidden in the forest, Murphy climbed a tree about 300 yards (275 meters) from the British unit. He spotted Fraser atop his horse, took careful aim, and fired. The single shot dropped the general. Murphy then delivered a second shot at another officer.

The British soldiers couldn't tell where the shots came from. Without their leaders, the soldiers retreated. They were later captured by other American forces.

HITTING AN ELEPHANT

By the Civil War, snipers knew to conceal themselves with clothing that differed from regular uniforms.

The shooting of Brigadier General Simon Fraser at the Battle of Bemis Heights in 1777 during the U.S. Revolutionary War was the first recorded death due to an American sniper's bullet.

Hiram Berdan was the commanding colonel of the United States Volunteer Sharpshooter Regiments. His snipers wore dark green uniforms with black trim. They also had gray felt hats and gray overcoats. The green blended in with leaves and other vegetation in spring and summer. The gray outerwear helped hide them in fall and winter.

The conflict saw snipers on both sides. They played key roles in such battles as the 1863 Battle of Gettysburg in Pennsylvania and the Battle of Spotsylvania Court House near Richmond, Virginia, in

A Confederate sniper shot Union general John Sedgwick in the Battle of Spotsylvania Court House during the American Civil War, depicted in this painting by Julian Scott.

1864. At Gettysburg, Union snipers fired from a ridge on the battlefield known as Devil's Den. Large boulders gave them cover until General Robert E. Lee's Southern troops attacked and won the day.

In the Battle of Spotsylvania Court House, Union general John Sedgwick had little respect for the Confederate sharpshooters positioned about 1,000 yards (914 meters) away. As Union troops took fire, they dived for cover. The general, mounted on his horse, wanted to encourage them. As reported in Charles Stronge's book *Kill Shot*, he shouted, "They couldn't hit an elephant at this distance!" Those were his last words. A round from a Rebel sniper hit him below his left eye.

IN THE TRENCHES

German snipers in World War I were better equipped and better trained than their Allied counterparts. German manufacturers had developed telescopic sights with high-quality lenses. The German army attached them to their rifles. The scopes made aiming at enemy soldiers much easier. Much of the war was fought in opposing trenches. German snipers watched and waited for an Allied soldier to poke his head above the trench to look at the battlefield. The sniper then picked him off.

At first, British and French soldiers thought the enemy just made lucky shots. Later, though, German rifles were recovered and the scopes examined. To provide better training for Allied soldiers, the British army started its own sniper school in 1916. Major

HISTORY'S BEST FEMALE SNIPER

Lyudmila Mykhailivna Pavlichenko is history's most successful female sniper. According to the book *Sniping: An Illustrated History*, in World War II she killed 309 German soldiers, including thirty-six enemy snipers.

She was born in Ukraine, and at age fourteen she joined an amateur shooting club in Kiev. She became skilled with a rifle. Years later, the Nazis invaded her country. She volunteered for the infantry and joined the Red Army's 25th Rifle Division.

When Lyudmila Mykhailivna Pavlichenko volunteered for the Russian army after the German invasion, she refused the recruiter's suggestion that she become a field nurse. Rather, Pavlichenko proved her shooting ability and joined as a shooter.

Near the end of the war, Pavlichenko trained other Soviet snipers. In 1943, she received the Gold Star of the Hero of the Soviet Union and was honored on a Soviet postage stamp. In 1976, two years after her death at the age of fifty-eight, a second Soviet stamp celebrated her achievements.

Hesketh Vernon Hesketh-Prichard founded the First Army School of Sniping, Observation, and Scouting at Linghem, France. He developed such modern sniping skills as observation, the use of spotting scopes, and working in pairs. Hesketh-Prichard later trained snipers from other Allied nations.

During World War II, sniper training for American forces focused on marksmanship. Little attention was paid to such activities as camouflage, observation, and stalking. Still, snipers played key roles in many battles.

U.S. Marine private Daniel Webster Cass Jr. fought on the Japanese island of Okinawa. In a battle called the Typhoon of Steel, his unit was pinned down by enemy machine gun fire. Cass and his spotter made their way to a ridge above the fighting. Fog and drizzle made finding the machine gun nest difficult. Finally, though, the spotter saw muzzle flashes and a thin trail of gun smoke coming from a well-hidden cave. The long-distance shot was difficult, but Cass placed his crosshairs on the enemy fighters and removed the machine gun's threat.

COLD WAR CONFLICTS

In the 1950s, the Democratic People's Republic of Korea (North Korea) invaded the Republic of Korea (South Korea). The United States and allies from the United Nations helped defend South Korea. Despite the damage caused by enemy snipers in both world wars, the U.S. military remained behind in sniper training compared to such nations as China and the Soviet Union, both of which supported North Korea.

American snipers worked mostly on marksmanship with little additional instruction. The Korean conflict emphasized the lack of American sniper talent. It also proved the importance of snipers in both attack and defense, as well as in action against enemy snipers.

Two decades later, U.S. Marine sergeant Carlos Hathcock served as a sniper in Vietnam. He was known not only for his accurate long-range shooting but also for his ability to hide, move undetected in a combat zone, and escape from the enemy after a shot. In one case, he was so well hidden that an enemy soldier nearly stepped on him without knowing he was there. His success finally taught the U.S. military the importance of snipers in modern warfare. Today their training is largely based on Hathcock's experience and skills.

SNIPERS IN THE MIDDLE EAST

During Operation Desert Storm in Iraq in the 1990s, U.S. snipers were better prepared than those snipers in previous conflicts. One of their tasks was to clear the enemy from such areas as the Al Wafrah forest, a farming area with small trees close to Iraq's oil fields. Alerted to a potential attack, American snipers lay in watch through the night to eliminate enemy soldiers.

Snipers were no less important in Afghanistan as they protected coalition troops. One stunning sniper shot stands out. On December 14, 2013, British soldiers at an observation post in Helmand Province saw a suspected Taliban suicide bomber and set out

American snipers who provided cover and observed enemy positions during the Persian Gulf War had better equipment and training than did their counterparts in earlier conflicts.

to stop him. During the resulting firefight, a British sniper a half mile (0.8 kilometers) away spotted a Taliban fighter armed with an AK47 assault rifle coming out of a ditch.

The sniper, unaware that the man was wearing a suicide vest, took aim and fired. The high-velocity bullet hit him in the torso and set off the vest's explosives. The resulting blast killed all six Taliban fighters. The unnamed sniper is credited with six hits from a single shot. He is also credited with stopping a major Taliban terrorist attack. In addition to the suicide vest that exploded, another one was found close to the action. It held forty-four pounds (twenty kilograms) of explosives.

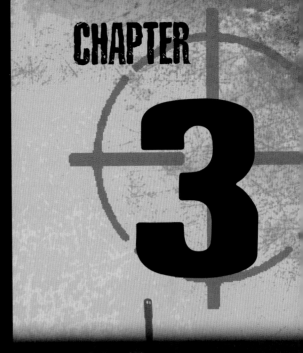

ENTRANCE EXAMS

Today's snipers are trained in special military or private schools that have stiff entrance requirements. The U.S. Army's Sniper School in Ft. Benning, Georgia, for example, requires candidates to be males in the infantry who are on active duty or in the U.S. Army National Guard or the U.S. Army Reserve. Would-be students need a good performance record with no disciplinary problems. Trainees must volunteer for the school and be recommended by their commanders.

After that, trainees must have earned a designation of "expert," the highest level of shooting ability, with the currently designated rifle. In addition, they must requalify each year. Candidates are examined for physical, mental, and emotional conditions. Results of a thorough psychological evaluation affect the selection process.

FIT TO SERVE

The sniper's physical condition and overall health must be outstanding. He needs good reflexes and muscle control as well as good stamina. The candidate must pass the Army Physical Fitness Test with a minimum score of seventy on each of three events: push-ups, sit-ups, and a timed 2-mile (3.2 km) run. Standards for each event vary by the soldier's age. A soldier who

Soldiers hoping to become military snipers face difficult and competitive entrance requirements including those for marksmanship, physical fitness, and psychological health and having no disciplinary issues on record.

developed self-confidence and body control from athletics is also a good prospect for sniper school.

A sniper trainee needs 20/20 vision or vision correctable to 20/20. However, wearing glasses may count against him. The lenses may reflect the sun and give away a position. Furthermore, if the glasses are lost or broken, the sniper's aim will suffer. However, contact lenses are allowed. Color-blindness is another negative factor. A sniper needs to be able to spot targets hidden by camouflage. The inability to distinguish certain colors makes that task difficult or impossible.

Trainees who apply to the U.S. Marines Corps Scout Sniper School must pass the Marine Corps Physical Fitness Test. A perfect score on the test requires a 3-mile (4.8-km) run in eighteen minutes, 20 dead-hang pull-ups, and 100 sit-ups in less than two minutes. The marines also require swimming qualifications of a 500-meter (1,640-foot) swim using sidestroke or breast-stroke, a 50-meter (164-foot) swim holding a weight out of water, and treading water holding a weight out of water for thirty seconds.

Trainees can have no history of alcohol or drug abuse. They can't use tobacco, either by smoking or chewing it. The smell of smoke or tobacco on clothing can give away the sniper's position even if he's not smoking during the mission. So can a smoker's cough. The temporary withdrawal from nicotine can make him nervous or irritable and lessen his ability.

Commanders who select sniper candidates look for such additional factors as reliability, intelligence,

TOP GUNS

Shooting competitions pit sniper teams against each other to hone skills they need on the battlefield. In 2013, for example, the National Guard Marksmanship Training Center at Camp Joseph T. Robinson in North Little Rock, Arkansas, hosted the 42nd Winston P. Wilson Sniper Championship at the Fort Chaffee Joint Maneuver Training Center near Fort Smith, Arkansas.

Snipers from fifteen two-man U.S. Army National Guard sniper teams competed in sixteen events to test their skills and weapon systems in conditions similar to those they might well face in combat. One event called a "heightened awareness situation" began at 6:30 AM after a night-firing exercise that ended at 5:00 AM. The men got only about an hour of sleep—the way they might on a battlefield.

After a fifteen-minute run through the woods to raise their heart rates, participants shot at targets amid simulated chaos. Instructors shouted at them and threw grenades of colored smoke, set grass fires near the firing positions, blasted air horns, and played loud Middle Eastern music to distract them. The snipers fired from standing, kneeling, and sitting positions with a limited number of rounds of ammunition. Judging was based on accuracy. Winning teams won bragging rights, but they also learned from each other during the contests.

The annual Winston P. Wilson Sniper Championship serves as a marksmanship training exercise. It matches military sniper teams from different U.S. Army National Guard units.

common sense, good judgment, and discipline. They also look for candidates with extensive outdoor experience. Some of the best snipers grew up in rural areas and are familiar with natural surroundings. Candidates for sniper school have an additional advantage if they are experienced game hunters.

GOING TO SCHOOL

Sniper schools are among the hardest schools anywhere. Graduates describe them as "intense" and "grueling," both mentally and physically. Many military branches offer sniper schools. So do private companies under contract to the U.S. government.

When a trainee is selected, the commander assigns which course he will attend and where. Four notable military schools include those run by the U.S. Army, U.S. Army National Guard, U.S. Marine Corps, and U.S. Navy. Some courses are offered in more than one location. And some schools train potential snipers from other military services.

Company D, 2nd Battalion 29th Infantry Regiment started the U.S. Army's first official sniper school in 1955, at the end of the Korean War. The present school was established at Fort Benning, Georgia, in 1987. It provides a seven-week course that includes stalking, marksmanship, night shooting, target detection, and estimation of the distance to a target. It requires fieldwork as well as written tests.

The Army National Guard Sniper School is held at Camp Joseph T. Robinson in central Arkansas, north of Little Rock. The course lasts five weeks (including weekends) and covers the same amount of work as the army's school, with the same entry requirements. Camp Robinson also hosts the U.S. Air Force's Countersniper School. The Marine Corps basic sniper school is located in Quantico, Virginia.

The U.S. Navy SEAL Sniper Schools on both the East and West coasts takes three months of twelve-hour days, seven days a week. Trainees need high intelligence because the training is so mentally tough.

"Sniper school is one of the very few courses a SEAL will not be looked down upon for failing to complete," says Brandon Webb, a former Navy SEAL and author of the *New York Times* best seller *The Red Circle*. "It's an unwritten rule that you don't give guys a hard time for washing out of sniper school. Because the course is known for its insane difficulty, just being selected or volunteering to go automatically elicits respect in the teams."

In Webb's class in 2000, for example, twenty-six started the course. Only twelve graduated.

A Special Operations Target Interdiction Course at Ft. Bragg, North Carolina, trains special operations personnel from all military branches, as well as those from other countries. It teaches advanced skills not covered in the other U.S. military courses.

SCHOOLS IN THE PRIVATE SECTOR

Some private sniper schools offer specialized training for particular purposes or specified weapons.

GPS DEFENSE

ABOUT US COURSES » FUNDING » EQUIPMENT » STORE FORUM MEDIA CONTACT

SNIPER COURSES

Experience the best sniper training and tactical precision rifle techniques taught anywhere!

...re

...om Remington 700 .308
J. Leupold, Remington &
...ua Authorized Dealer,
...ing kits & much more.

Sniper Rifles

Our rifles are custom designed based upon our school's 15-year experience teaching hundreds of students.

Sniper Courses

Experience the best sniper training and tactical precision rifle techniques taught anywhere!

Medical Training

Scenario Based Tactical Emergency Casualty Care (TECC) Training – AZ POST Approved

GPS Defense operates a comprehensive school for military and law enforcement snipers near Phoenix, Arizona. Its facilities include shooting ranges, a desert village, moving targets, stalk lanes, and urban training.

The U.S. Training Center, operated by Academi on a 7,000-acre (2,833-hectare) facility in Moyock, North Carolina, offers Military Mobile Force Protection Training. The course focuses on enhancing the survivability of special operations forces in both urban and rural environments. Although the course was developed for use in Iraq and Afghanistan, the training also applies to other high-threat situations.

The GPS Defense Sniper School in Scottsdale, Arizona, offers such courses as Sniper/Counter Sniper, Advanced Sniper, and Sniper Instructor Development. Trainees include civilians and law enforcement personnel, as well as military personnel. Other private schools focus on such topics as basic fundamentals, advanced marksmanship, and long-range rifle training.

TRAINING DAYS

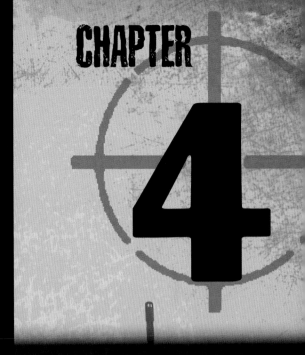

Trainees who think getting into sniper school is hard soon learn that completing the training is even harder. The two main parts of sniper schools are shooting and fieldcraft. The shooting phase covers learning about weapons, advanced ballistics, and marksmanship. Fieldcraft includes camouflage, observation, and stalking. And physical fitness training means 6-mile (9.7 km) runs in the morning, marches carrying 60-pound (27 kg) packs, and strength-building sit-ups and push-ups. Snipers train to be both shooters and spotters and may serve in either role according to the mission.

Author and former Navy Seal sniper Brandon Webb described the school he attended on NavySeal.com. "Our training demands that every graduate be one of a unique breed, willing to snake his way through treacherous urban war-zone terrain or crawl the hot desert floor for hours, slow as a snail . . . sometimes withstanding days on end of unendurable physical hardship to set up on his target," he said. "Still, the physical ability is maybe ten percent of it. Most of it is mental."

INSTRUCTION

During the first part of sniper schools, instructors teach mental preparation and how to construct a hide for a firing position. Along with firing-range practice, trainees learn about the effects of wind and gravity, and how to measure accuracy. The shooting phase of training includes lessons in ballistics and the capabilities of different types of ammunition. Trainees learn how to adjust such optical devices as rifle scopes, spotter scopes, and night vision equipment. They're taught about rifle selection and maintenance, scoped rifle marksmanship, shot placement, and nighttime shooting techniques.

The first phase of training also covers land navigation skills, data logging, record keeping, and intelligence gathering and photography. In addition to knowing about allied troops' firearms and equipment, snipers must learn to identify enemy uniforms, weapons, and gear.

Because communication with their commander is critical, snipers must know how to operate radio equipment, as well as the procedures for using it. They also learn what to look for as they observe mortar and artillery fire in case the need arises to adjust the aim of the heavy equipment.

DETERMINING WIND VELOCITY

To adjust the sights on sniper weapons, shooters must know wind speed and direction, both of which affect accuracy. According to the U.S. Army's Field Manual 23-10, the trainee uses such indicators as range flags, smoke, trees, grass, rain, and the feeling on his skin.

During training, a sniper watches a flag on the shooting range. He figures the angle between the flag and the flagpole in degrees. He divides that number by four. The answer gives him a good estimate of wind velocity in miles per hour. Instead of using a flag, the sniper can also drop such light material as paper, grass, or cotton from shoulder level. He points at the object on the ground and figures the angle between his arm and body. Again dividing by four, he gets the approximate wind speed in miles per hour.

To aim at a target precisely, a sniper uses various methods to determine wind velocity in the area. Wind affects the way a bullet travels through the air.

The initial training is so difficult that many trainees fail. In an article for the Department of Defense, Bob Haskell writes about one Army National Guard sniper school: "Twenty-one reported for the first two weeks of marksmanship training . . . Eleven graduated and earned the right to return [for more training]."

THE ART OF OBSERVATION

Trainees who pass the first phase of instruction move on to an advanced program. Sometimes these skills are taught at the same location or at a series of separate schools. These advanced skills include advanced camouflage and concealment, long-range shooting, sniper assaults, ambush drills, and night movement and shooting. It may also include drills to teach the skills needed to protect persons of high rank or office.

Moving target shooting is usually taught in this part of the school. Snipers use two ways to aim at a moving target. One is called the tracking method. The sniper puts the gun sight's crosshairs on the target and follows him through the scope as he moves. The other is called the ambush method—or leading the target. With the latter method, the sniper aims ahead of the target in the direction the target is moving. The sniper waits to fire until the target gets to the crosshairs.

Important parts of this phase of instruction are field-training exercises that involve extreme stress and physical effort. Field exercises include lessons in observation. One such exercise is the KIMS game.

English author Rudyard Kipling described the game in his 1901 novel, *Kim*. The game was used to train British snipers during World War I by sniper school founder Major Hesketh Hesketh-Prichard. American military sniper schools, including the U.S. Marine Corps Scout Sniper School, still use the KIMS game. The game is commonly called the "keep in memory system," but its name first referred to Kipling's character.

In the KIMS game, trainees look at ten to twenty objects laid out on a table for a short period of time—perhaps sixty seconds. The collection may include

SCHMIDT ⊙ BENDER

As many of their assignments involve surveillance of enemy unit strength, equipment, and position, snipers need exceptional observational skills. They train to notice anything that seems out of place.

such items as a paper clip, bottle top, bullet, and pencil. Trainees then must describe what they saw. They may not, however, name the objects.

In his article "How Military Snipers Work," Robert Valdes quotes an unnamed source he refers to as Army Ranger Sniper. "You weren't allowed to say 'paper clip,'" the source reports. "You'd have to say, 'silver, metal wire, bent in two oval shapes.' They want the Intel guys making the decision about what you actually saw."

Instructors repeat the KIMS game many times during the course, adding more objects and giving trainees less time to look at them and more time between viewing and telling what they saw. As the game progresses, the objects may be seen first thing in the morning and not recalled until after an entire day of training.

Another observation exercise is conducted on an open field. Instructors hide things and trainees then use scopes to find them in a specified time. To accomplish the task, a trainee stares through a scope at a certain spot for several minutes. He then moves the scope to a new place for a minute or two more. Trainees learn to look for things that don't make sense or appear out of place.

SNEAKING AROUND

Stalk training teaches stealth, the art of cautious movement. Instructors also use another challenging "game." Trainees start at one end of an open grassy range while two instructors with spotter scopes watch from an elevated position or tower 1,094 yards (1,000 meters) away. The goal is to move to within 164 yards (150 meters) of the instructors without being seen. But the instructors aren't the only ones looking for the stalkers. Two more soldiers serve as "walkers," who stay in radio contact with the instructors down range. The walkers move around the field looking for the stalkers, too.

When the stalker reaches the correct distance, he shoots one blank at the instructors. The stalker then moves to a second firing position and shoots again. During the exercise, the instructors hold up a certain number of fingers. Stalkers must record the correct number of fingers to prove where they aimed. The shots must be carefully taken. If the instructors see a muzzle flash or kicked-up dirt from a miss, the stalker's position will be revealed.

Test standards are tough. Stalkers either pass or fail this exercise, which is repeated again and again throughout the course of training at school. Too many failures and the student must leave the program.

CHAPTER 5

TOOLS OF THE TRADE

Snipers use only items that are absolutely necessary for each mission. But that doesn't mean they travel light. They need weapons, scopes, ammunition, a radio, and a wide variety of other equipment and gear. They must also take their own food and water.

A sniper's firearm is called a weapon system because it has a detachable telescopic sight as well as other accessories. Snipers sometimes use semi-automatic rifles, but they usually use bolt-action ones. Bolt-action rifles require the shooter to load each round separately. Likewise, the spent cartridge must be removed by hand. This helps the sniper remain hidden. A semi-automatic flings the spent cartridge into the air—motion an enemy could notice and find the sniper's position.

Bolt-action rifles are harder to use than semi-automatic rifles, but they have fewer moving parts. That means they can be quickly broken down and reassembled. They are reliable and accurate. And they are usually lighter and less expensive than self-loading firearms.

WEAPON SYSTEMS

In 2011, the U.S. Army introduced the XM2010 enhanced sniper rifle in Afghanistan. The rifle has a detachable sound suppressor for missions that

According to the U.S. Army, sniper teams in Afghanistan used the XM2010 weapon system, an upgraded M24 system that increased the sniper's effective range by 50 percent.

require silence. The suppressor significantly reduces muzzle flash as well as sound to help the shooter avoid detection.

Sniper rifles have high-tech mounted scopes to make aiming easier and more accurate. To get the most out of each shot, a sniper needs to know the effects of external factors on each shot. One such factor, called bullet drop, is the amount of change in the round's path due to wind, gravity, temperature, and motion of the target. Another effect is spin drift, which changes a bullet's path because of its upward roll when fired. The sniper must be aware of these effects and adjust his aim accordingly.

In some cases, precise calculations are required. However, modern computerized scopes such as a smart scope manufactured by the TrackingPoint Company collects information about external factors and compensates for them before the sniper fires.

The XM2010 first came fitted with a Leupold Mark 4 telescopic sight (manufactured by the Leupold & Stevens company). However, in March 2014 the TrackingPoint Company announced that its smart scope was being added to the rifle after the army successfully tested it earlier in the year.

The computerized scope has sensors that collect information about external factors. The sniper then marks the target and the scope accounts for such variables as wind, weather, and even the earth's rotation. The scope takes that information, calculates it as needed, and then adjusts the system. A specialized trigger won't let the rifle fire until the aim is correct. The smart scope's wireless computer can send information to a laptop, smart phone, or tablet computer for spotting purposes or for sharing intelligence.

The new scope gives the system a 1,250-yard (1,143-meter) effective range. Effective range is the farthest distance a soldier can expect his shot to hit the target. For missions in mountain and desert areas, the longer the range, the better.

Although views using night-vision technology aren't as clear as in daylight, sniper teams with night-vision goggles and weapon system gun sights "own the night" in observation and combat missions after dark.

OPTIMUM OPTICS AND OTHER EQUIPMENT AND GEAR

Sniper teams use a variety of optical devices to improve their ability to clearly see and aim at targets. In addition to the scope on the rifle, teams use observation telescopes, binoculars, and night-vision goggles.

Sniper teams use an observation telescope for all missions. For example, the U.S. Army's M49 observation telescope enlarges distant objects twenty times. It shows more detail than can be seen with the naked eye. The telescope helps the sniper team's spotter to figure wind speed and direction and to watch a bullet's flight path and impact. It also helps him see camouflaged, shadowy, or moving targets.

Binoculars improve viewing in low-light conditions. They are used for the hasty search observation technique and to select and estimate the distance to a target. Snipers also use them to observe target areas as well as enemy positions and movement. On occasion, a sniper team may ask for indirect fire on a specific area. Indirect fire is firing without a direct line of sight to the target. It is commonly used for field artillery, mortars, and machine guns. The spotter uses binoculars to see where the shots fall and to provide adjustments for shots that miss.

Night-vision goggles increase light from the moon or stars to help snipers observe areas in darkness. Views through the goggles aren't as clear as in daylight, but they help snipers perform their observation role at night. The shooting member of a sniper team carries the goggles because the spotter has a night-vision sight on his weapon system. Shooters don't use night-vision gun sights because of their limited range.

Snipers must stay in touch with their commander and all units participating in the mission. Each team carries a lightweight portable radio designed for fast and easy use. Radios operate for voice, Morse code, or digital data, and can be tuned to different frequencies as needed.

In addition to the sniper weapon system, each sniper team member needs a sidearm (that is, a handgun) for protection from threats at close range. Each team member carries a compass and a rucksack with food, a two-quart canteen, a first-aid kit, pruning shears to cut vegetation, a sewing kit, and extra netting to build a hide or to repair the ghillie suit. The ghillie suit itself is stored in the rucksack when not being worn.

The team also needs military maps of the area, a pocket-sized calculator, and a 10-foot to 25-five-foot (3 to 7.6 m) metal carpenter's tape. They use the tape to measure items close to their position for recording in a sniper data book. The sniper data book contains a written record of everything that happens in the team's area in the order in which it happens. It gives commanders and intelligence personnel an idea of what an area looks like and a record of the activity there. The book holds data cards, where the snipers record results of shots taken. It also records the factors that affect the firing of the weapon—from the weather to the shooter's attitude. The sniper uses this

WHAT A WELL-DRESSED U.S. NAVY SEAL SNIPER WEARS TO WORK

According to the U.S. Navy Seal Sniper Training Program, the following list includes "essential equipment" for a sniper mission. Such additional equipment as swim fins may be required depending on the target, area, entrance and escape routes, and other elements of the plan.

- Uniform suitable for terrain and climate
- Remington Model 700 .300 Winchester Magnum (Win Mag) rifle
- MX-300R or MX-360 hand radio
- Spotting scope
- Binoculars
- Map of area
- Log book if working in a sniper team
- Range card
- Range finder
- Forty rounds 7.62 or .300 Win Mag ammunition
- Standard issue sidearm with thirty rounds
- Red-lens flashlight
- Night-vision scopes for night missions
- Secondary weapon with M-845 night vision device

information to learn more about his weapon system as well as what factors affect his shooting ability under a variety of conditions.

Another important record is the range card. The range card shows a bird's-eye view of a target area. Preprinted rings on the card give the sniper a quick distance reference, as well as a way to record target locations. The team notes its position and the distances to roads, structures, and any physical features of the land. The range card includes places to add distance and elevation, as well as wind, temperature, and target reference points.

It's important to note that these "tools of the trade" are often replaced by newer models, since the U.S. military often updates and changes sources for weapons and other equipment with additional capabilities.

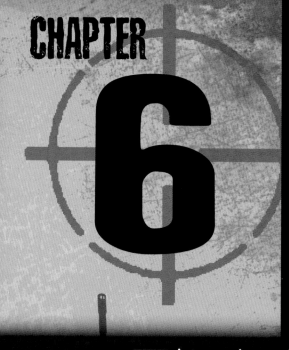

CHAPTER 6

GOING THE DISTANCE

Distance is a sniper's friend. The farther he is from the target, the harder it is for the enemy to shoot back, and the better the chance he has of leaving the firing position in safety. But distance can also hamper the sniper's job. The farther a bullet travels, the more such factors as wind, elevation, and temperature affect its path. That's why snipers are considered high-precision weapons in and of themselves.

As of 2014, the world's longest sniper shot occurred in Afghanistan in November 2009. Conditions were perfect for a long-range shot. Weather was clear and mild with no wind. British Corporal of Horse Craig Harrison was providing over-watch for an Afghan national army patrol near Musa Qala in Helmand Province. Taliban machine-gunners were firing on the patrol, and Harrison sought to take them out.

He fired nine shots to help figure out the distance to the targets, while his spotter Cliff O'Farrell reported results of each shot. The targets were 1,000 yards (914 meters) farther than the recommended range of the Accuracy International L115A3 long-range rifle Harrison had.

Harrison fired three shots. Each round took close to three seconds to reach the target. Harrison dropped both machine-gunners and destroyed one of the machine guns. One of the shots went more than a mile and a half. According to Guinness World

A British sniper observes the scene during a fierce battle between coalition troops and Taliban fighters near Musa Qala in Helmand Province, Afghanistan, where history's longest sniper shot occurred.

Records, which recognized the shot as the longest sniper shot in history, the range was 2,707 yards (2,475 meters), confirmed by the space-based satellite navigation system GPS.

LONG SHOTS

U.S. Marine gunnery sergeant Carlos Hathcock II used a .50 caliber M2 Browning machine gun for his record-setting 2,500-yard (2,286-meter) shot in Vietnam in 1967. The record stood for thirty-five years. As of 2014, it still ranked as the fifth-longest sniper shot in history.

However, Hathcock's most famous shot happened a year earlier in the jungle near Hill 55, an artillery firing area southwest of Da Nang. He and his spotter John Rolland Burke were stalking an enemy sniper known as the Cobra, who had already killed several U.S. Marines. By that time, Hathcock had developed a reputation as an accurate sniper himself, and some think the Cobra was sent to target him.

After Gunnery Sergeant Carlos Norman Hathcock II (right) retired, he was awarded the Silver Star Medal, the U.S. military's third-highest decoration for valor, for his "gallantry in action" in Vietnam.

WHITE FEATHER

His fellow soldiers called him "Gunny." The enemy nicknamed him "White Feather" because he always wore a white feather on his bush cap. The story of Gunnery Sergeant Carlos Norman Hathcock II is a U.S. Marine Corps legend.

He enlisted in the marines in 1959 and qualified as an expert marksman during boot camp. Three years later at the USMC Air Station in Cherry Point, North Carolina, he scored 248 out of a possible 250 on the "A" course. Years later when the marines stopped using the course, Hathcock's record still stood.

In 1965, Hathcock became a Marine Corps Distinguished Sniper. That year he also won the Wimbledon Cup, a marksmanship trophy (not to be confused with the tennis award), in the 1,000-yard (914-meter) shooting match at the National High-Power Rifle Championship at Camp Perry, Ohio.

He served two tours in Vietnam and had ninety-three confirmed enemy kills. However, estimates put the actual count at more than 300. He did so much damage to the enemy that the North Vietnamese army offered an award to anyone who killed him. Such awards were not uncommon. But at a time when the typical bounty on American snipers was usually anywhere between the U.S. equivalent of $8.00 and $2,000, the $30,000 award put on Hathcock's head shows how feared he was.

Both snipers were aware of each other as they circled through the jungle. Hathcock was settled into a firing position when he saw a reflection of light in the dense vegetation. Hathcock fired. His shot went straight through the enemy's riflescope. The Cobra had been mere seconds from doing the same to Hathcock.

MORE CRACK SHOTS

Of the top five sniper shots in history, only one, by Gunnery Sergeant Hathcock, occurred in Vietnam. The rest were recorded in Iraq and Afghanistan thirty-five or more years later. The new distance records are due in part to better training, but also to new technology, which improved equipment. The new weapon systems had greater range and accuracy in the hands of skilled shooters.

The second- and third-longest sniper shots in history came from Canadian snipers serving in the same sniper group in Afghanistan. In 2002, they broke Hathcock's Vietnam record twice within a matter of weeks. Master Corporal Arron Perry was supporting soldiers from the U.S. 101st Airborne Division during Operation Anaconda. Al-Qaeda fighters had them pinned down in the Shah-i-Kot Valley. Perry fired a McMillan Brothers Tac-50 bolt-action rifle to eliminate an al-Qaeda combatant 2,526 yards (2,310 meters) away.

Corporal Rob Furlong and his spotter were attached to the same American forces during that same operation. Just weeks after Perry broke

Hathcock's long-standing record, Furlong saw three al-Qaeda fighters moving up a mountain to establish a firing position. One carried a Kalashnikov handheld machine gun known in Russian as the Ruchnoy Pulemyot Kalashnikova. Americans call it the RPK. The Soviet-designed weapon was first manufactured in the 1950s for the Red Army.

Furlong used the same type of McMillan Brothers Tac-50 rifle as his countryman. He aimed at the fighter carrying the machine gun. The first shot missed. The second hit the target's backpack. The third eliminated him. The rounds each took nearly four seconds to travel the range of 2,657 yards (2,430 meters) to erase Perry's distance record.

American Sergeant Brian Kremer from the U.S. Army's 2nd Ranger Battalion took the fifth-longest shot during the war in Iraq in 2004. He used a Barrett M82A1 semi-automatic .50 caliber rifle for the hit that carried 2,515 yards (2,300 meters).

All of the top five listed distances have been confirmed. One that isn't listed, however, may break Harrison's world record. Chris Masters writing for the *Daily Telegraph* in Sydney, Australia, reported that an unknown Australian in the Australian Army's Delta Company, 2nd Commando Regiment made a 3,079-yard (2,815-meter) shot in Afghanistan in October 2012. According to the report, he used a .50 caliber Barrett M82 rifle. Neither the Australian army nor the Australian government has verified the report.

THE DEER HUNTER:
ONE MORE NOTABLE SHOT

Jim Gilliland's 1,367-yard (1,250-meter) shot in Iraq in 2005 was remarkable not only for distance but also because of the weapon he used. The staff sergeant led the U.S. 3rd Infantry Division's Sniper Shadow Team, a ten-man sniper unit. During a firefight in Ramadi in 2005, Gilliland was in an over-watch position on a rooftop protecting American troops.

Just after an enemy sniper killed an American soldier, Gilliland set about looking for the shooter. He spotted the enemy holding an RPK on a fourth-floor

Snipers don't always need high-tech equipment to land a shot. A U.S. sniper in Iraq used a standard-issue M24 rifle to eliminate a target 1,367 yards (1,250 meters) away.

balcony of a hospital more than thirteen football fields away.

Gilliland had no high-tech sniper weapon—only the standard-issue M24 rifle. Civilian deer hunters know the weapon as the .308 Winchester. Gilliland had hunted deer in his home state of Alabama before joining the military, so he was familiar with his rifle's capability. He thought he had no hope of taking out the sniper. His target stood well beyond the rifle's Leupold sight, which was thought to be accurate only up to 1,094 yards (1,000 meters).

Still, he wanted at least to scare off the sniper from the balcony. Gilliland adjusted his aim. He placed his crosshairs twelve feet above and eight feet to the left of the target and fired. His shot had to fall just right, and it did. He killed the enemy sniper.

ALL IN A DAY'S (OR NIGHT'S) WORK

Despite these better-known sniper shots, most snipers' work happens without media coverage or heroes' welcomes. Their job is to protect their troops. They use specialized training for dangerous missions to spy on the enemy and then report back to their commanders. When necessary, they use precision long-range fire to intimidate the enemy and remove potential threats. With fine-tuned skills and increasingly high-tech equipment, the American snipers of Special Ops are among the deadliest weapons in modern warfare.

GLOSSARY

AMBUSH METHOD A way to shoot at a moving target by aiming ahead of the direction the target is moving and waiting until the target arrives at the spot; also called "leading the target."

ARMORED PERSONNEL CARRIER A vehicle used to carry troops on a battlefield.

BALLISTICS The science of firearms and projectiles, particularly the firing, flight, and effects of ammunition.

BULLET DROP The amount of change in a bullet's path due to gravity, wind, or other factors.

CAMOUFLAGE The disguise of personnel or equipment by painting or covering them so that they blend in with the surrounding area.

COLLATERAL DAMAGE Unnecessary and unintended damage to civilians during an attack on an enemy.

CORPORAL OF HORSE A rank in the British army's Household Cavalry; it falls above sergeant and below staff sergeant.

CROSSHAIRS A pair of perpendicular wires or thin lines in a gun sight used to aim at a target.

EFFECTIVE RANGE The farthest distance a soldier can expect his shot to hit the target.

FIELDCRAFT The skills needed to work in open country without being seen.

GHILLIE SUIT A disguise made of uniform overalls or shirt and pants and covered with netting and jute or other plant fibers to help a sniper blend in with the environment.

HIDE The location where snipers position themselves to observe an area or to engage a target without being seen; also called the final firing position, or FFP.

IMPROVISED EXPLOSIVE DEVICE (IED) A homemade bomb often used as a roadside bomb.

INDIRECT FIRE Firing without a direct line of sight to the target; commonly used for field artillery, mortars, and machine guns.

INFANTRY Soldiers in an army who are trained and equipped with small arms to march and fight on foot.

OVER-WATCH Observation that supports a military unit from a higher position to provide cover or support during military activity.

SKYLINING The outlining of a person above the horizon, making the person an easy target.

SNIPER A skilled shooter who observes and/or fires at enemy soldiers or targeted objects from a concealed place.

SPIN DRIFT The amount of change in a bullet's path due to its upward roll in the direction of the spin when fired.

SPLASH The dirt or other material kicked up by a bullet when it hits the ground.

SPOTTER A sniper-team observer who helps the shooter with target selection and adjustments in sighting a weapon.

STALKING Pursuing or approaching a target without being seen or heard, using movements that include quietly walking as well as crawling.

SWIRL The vapor trail of a bullet caused by the displacement of air in the bullet's path.

TARGET INDICATOR Anything a sniper does that could result in detection or give away his location.

TRACKING METHOD A way to aim at a moving target by putting the gun sight's crosshairs on him and then following that person through the scope.

WEAPON SYSTEM A sniper rifle fitted with a detachable telescopic sight and other accessories.

FOR MORE INFORMATION

American Sniper Association
6232 Apple Road
Sebring, FL 33875
(863) 385-7835
E-mail: info@americansniper.org
Website: http://www.americansniper.org

The American Sniper Association works to improve the image, abilities, proficiency, and safety of professional snipers. It provides education, and supports and shares information with law enforcement agencies and military units.

American Snipers.Org
SOL/AS.org
101 S Military Avenue, Suite P211
Green Bay, WI 54303-2409
Website: http://www.americansnipers.org/content.php?113

American Snipers.Org is a nonprofit organization that began in 2003 as the Adopt a Sniper program, a support network of American police SWAT team snipers who supported American military snipers overseas. Membership now includes both law enforcement and military snipers.

Army Sniper Association
Attn: Candyss Bryant
P.O. Box 201676
Austin, TX 78720
(706) 718-9520
Website: http://www.armysniper.org

The Army Sniper Association is a nonprofit organization that seeks to create friendships among past and present snipers and to nurture the idea of the sniper in the active military. Through partnerships with individuals and corporations, the organization also works to help wounded snipers and their families, as well as families of snipers killed in action.

Operational Shooting Association
P.O. Box 275
Kinmount, ON, K0M 2A0
Canada
E-mail: ExecutiveDirector@osacanada.ca
Website: http://www.osacanada.ca

Members of the Operational Shooting Association include law enforcement and military personnel, as well as civilians. The group offers practices, training clinics, and competitions for service pistols, tactical rifles, and sniper precision rifles.

WEBSITES

Because of the changing nature of Internet links, Rosen Publishing has developed an online list of websites related to the subject of this book. This site is updated regularly. Please use this link to access the list:

http://www.rosenlinks.com/ISF/Snip

FOR FURTHER READING

Bowen, Carl. *Shadow Squadron*. North Mankato, MN: Capstone Young Readers, 2013.

David, Jack. *Marine Corps Force Recon*. Minneapolis, MN: Bellwether Media, 2009.

Earl, C. F., and Gabrielle Vanderhoof. *Army Rangers*. Broomall, PA: Mason Crest, 2011.

Gregory, Josh. *Special Ops*. North Mankato, MN: Cherry Lake Publishing, 2013.

Lusted, Marcia Amidon. *Army Delta Force*. Minneapolis, MN: Lerner Publishing Group, 2013.

Lusted, Marcia Amidon. *Army Rangers: Elite Operations*. Minneapolis, MN: Lerner Publishing Group, 2013.

Lusted, Marcia Amidon. *Marine Force Recon*. Minneapolis, MN: Lerner Publishing Group, 2013.

Lynch, Chris. *Vietnam Sharpshooter*. New York, NY: Scholastic Press, 2012.

Montana, Jack. *Elite Forces Selection*. Broomall, PA: Mason Crest, 2011.

Newman, Patricia. *Army Special Forces: Elite Operations*. Minneapolis, MN: Lerner Publishing Group, 2013.

Person, Stephen. *Navy SEAL Team Six in Action*. New York, NY: Bearport Publishing, 2013.

Riordan, James. *The Sniper*. London, England: Frances Lincoln Children's Books, 2009.

Rudolf, Jessica, and Fred Pushies. *Marine Scout Snipers in Action*. New York, NY: Bearport Publishing, 2013.

Sizer, Mona D. *The Glory Days: The Story of the U.S. Army Rangers*. Lanham, MD: Taylor Trade Publishing, 2010.

BIBLIOGRAPHY

American Heroes Channel. "Modern Warfare: Top Ten Snipers." Retrieved February 22, 2014 (http://www.ahctv.com/modern-warfare/10-snipers.htm).

Cavallaro, Gina, and Matt Larsen. *Sniper: American Single-Shot Warriors in Iraq and Afghanistan*. Guilford, CT: Lyons Press, 2010.

Haskell, Bob. "National Guard Sniper School." Department of Defense. Retrieved April 8, 2014 (http://usmilitary.about.com/od/guardandreserve/l/blsniperschool.htm).

Lynn, Brian. "Eight Longest Sniper Shots in History." *Guns and Ammo*, September 27, 2011. Retrieved February 27, 2014 (http://www.gunsandammo.com/2011/09/27/longest-sniper-shots-in-history).

U.S. Army. *Field Manual 23-10*. BiblioGov, October 18, 2012. Retrieved April 6, 2014 (http://pdf.textfiles.com/manuals/MILITARY/united_states_army_fm_23-10%20-%2017_august_1994.pdf).

U.S. Navy. *U.S. Navy Seal Sniper Training Program*. New York, New York: Skyhorse Publishing Inc., 2011.

Valdes, Robert. "How Military Snipers Work." Science.HowStuffWorks.com.Retrieved April 11, 2014 (http://science.howstuffworks.com/sniper10.htm).

Webb, Brandon. "Navy SEAL Sniper School." NavySEALs.com, January 18, 2013. Retrieved April 8, 2014 (http://navyseals.com/1556/navy-seal-sniper-school-part-1/0).

INDEX

ABOUT THE AUTHOR

Mary-Lane Kamberg, a professional writer, editor, and speaker, is the author of twenty books for young readers. She specializes in nonfiction, but she has also published poetry and short fiction. Her husband served in the U.S. Navy, and as a navy wife she accompanied him to duty stations at Naval Station Roosevelt Roads in Puerto Rico and Naval Station Norfolk in Virginia.

PHOTO CREDITS